The Joy
of Cats

by Jo Kittinger

ⓜ Meadowbrook Press

Distributed by Simon & Schuster
New York

Library of Congress Cataloging-in-Publication Data

Kittinger, Jo S.
    The joy of cats / by Jo Kittinger.
        p.   cm.
    ISBN 0-88166-337-9 (mb).—ISBN 0-671-31726-1 (S&S)
    1. Cats Quotations, maxims, etc. I. Title.
PN6084.C23K585   1999
636.8—dc21   99-27367
                                              CIP

Editor: Bruce Lansky
Coordinating Editors: Joseph Gredler, Heather Hooper, and Jason Sanford
Production Manager: Joe Gagne
Production Assistant: Danielle White
Cover Photography *(clockwise from top left corner):* © TSM/Roy Morsch;
© T. Rosenthal/SuperStock; © W. Adams/SuperStock; © Visual Horizons/FPG Int.;
© Gary Randall/FPG Int.; © John Cajda/FPG Int.

Published by Meadowbrook Press, 5451 Smetana Drive, Minnetonka, MN 55343
www.meadowbrookpress.com

BOOK TRADE DISTRIBUTION by Simon & Schuster, a division of Simon and Schuster, Inc.,
1230 Avenue of the Americas, New York, NY 10020

03 02 01 00 99   10 9 8 7 6 5 4 3 2 1

Printed in the United States of America

Introduction

In this dog-eat-dog world, there is solace to be found in one's cats. Cats provide quiet companionship, incredible entertainment, and a soft warm fuzzy when you need it most.

I have always loved animals of all sorts. Over the years, I've shared my home with dogs, hamsters, gerbils, rats, guinea pigs, rabbits, a monkey, a dove, fish, snakes, lizards, turtles, and a ferret. Each pet had qualities I enjoyed. However, each had other characteristics I found less than lovable. My cats, on the other hand, have brought me nothing but joy.

I say nothing but joy because love is blind. Of course my cats have shredded the furniture, killed other critters, and left fur on every conceivable surface. As with my children, I overlook the shortcomings of my cats because they bring me such joy.

Our home was blessed with a litter of four kittens just last night. Although I agree that the world doesn't need another litter when there are so many homeless pets, I can't apologize for the happiness I feel. I know my world will be special for the next eight weeks as I frolic with these kittens.

Those of you who are "cat people" will smile and nod as you recognize your own pets and feelings in these quotes. A great deal of time was spent trying to capture the essence of the joy cats bring. So cuddle up with a cat and enjoy!

Jo S. Kittinger

Acknowledgments

We would like to thank the individuals who served on a reading panel for this project: Reggie Anderson, Ken Bastien, Ricki Block, Elizabeth Bolton, Tamera L. Collins, Shannon Compton, Eileen Daily, Wendy Fitter, Carole Goggin, Babs Bell Hajdusiewicz, Dick Hayman, Jill Hilpert, Joan Horton, Ellen Jackson, Wendy Lees, Ann Lynch, Ingrid McCleary, Julie Mieseler, Barbara Merchant, Rolaine Merchant, Ruth Moose, Margaret Park Bridges, Renee Paulson, C. Pleasants York, Heidi Roemer, Jerry Rosen, Lawrence Schimel, Rosemary J. Schmidt, Patti Schnetzler, Michele Smith, Janet Thamus, Amy Unger, Vicki Wiita

We would also like to thank the photographers who contributed to this book: p. 14 © TSM/Joan Baron; p. 21 © TSM/Roy Morsch; pp. 2 and 9 © Robert C. Hayes; p. 35 © Camerique/Index Stock Imagery; p. 90 © Carl Vanderschuit/Index Stock Imagery; p. 26 © Robert Firth/Firth Photobank; p. 38 © Robert Firth/Firth Photobank; p. 80 © Paul Sinkler/Firth Photobank; p. 54 © W. Adams/SuperStock; p. 61 © T. Rosenthal/SuperStock; p. 97 © K. Coppieters/SuperStock; p. 47 © John Cajda/FPG Int.; pp. 68 and 75 © Gary Randall/FPG Int.; p. 85 © Diane Padys/ FPG Int.; p. 100 © Visual Horizons/FPG Int.

Dedication

I dedicate this book to my children, Michael, Robert, and Rebecca, who love animals as much as I do. How precious are the memories and the photos I have of you curled up with our sweet cats.

And to our golden retriever, Solomon, who kindly puts up with our cats' affection.

An ordinary cat can make an
ordinary life extraordinary.

Life is hard. Soften yours with a cat.

Happiness does not light gently on
my shoulder like a butterfly. She pounces
on my lap, demanding that I scratch
behind her ears.

In that moment when you first
see the litter, your eyes meet
and you know that tiny kitten
is meant to be part of your life.

Companionship is right under your feet
when you own a cat.

Owning a cat is like reading a good
novel—just when you think you know the
main character, she'll surprise you on the
very next page.

You'll never cry over spilt milk
if you own a cat.

Cats are so simple. They need no instructions—just food, litter, and love.

The thrill of owning cats is not in some benefit or service provided, but simply in the fact that such an awesome creature would consent to share your life.

Owning a cat is a good forerunner of marriage. You learn that you cannot control another living being, or expect him to do everything you want.

Sometimes a cat is like your
grandmother's quilt—it keeps you warm,
tucked in with memories and love.

When the temperature plunges,
I snuggle with my calico cat.
She's like a miniature crazy quilt.

Cats are like your favorite robe—
soft, warm, and fuzzy.

It warms my heart when I come in
from the cold and my cat meets me
at the door.

When a blizzard knocks the power out,
it's good to have warm furry friends.

On a cold winter night a furry, purry
heating pad comes in handy.

My cat has one ability.
No sense of it I make.
How is it he falls fast asleep
yet keeps his ears awake?

A cat prefers the softest bed but will sleep
wherever you lay your head.

You never get up on the wrong side
of the bed when a purring cat sleeps
by your head.

It is said that Muhammad once cut off
part of his robe to avoid disturbing his
cat's slumber. I would simply have
waited for the cat to wake up.

A sleeping cat is a good excuse not to
make the bed.

Birds have nests and foxes have dens.
Cats have laundry baskets full of freshly
washed clothes.

I feel much better about my lazy habits
when I see how cozy my cat is
curled up on a pile of dirty clothes.

Sometimes your cat wakes you in the middle of the night. But remember you also wake her in the middle of the day.

A cat asleep in your lap is the perfect excuse for not doing the dishes.

A cat in the lap; time for a nap.

Running your fingers through the fur
of a cat is as delightful as walking
barefoot in the grass.

Cats are furry. Cats are fun.
I think I want another one.

A mongrel cat snuggles and purrs
just as well as a show cat.

A cat makes sure you're never
lonely, even when you're
brushing your teeth.

Cats fill the empty spaces in your heart.

Blessed are those who love cats,
for they shall never be lonely.

The blackest cat on the darkest night
can add a little light to your life.

Remember, cats can see in the dark. So
when there is no sunshine in your life,
your cat can still find and comfort you.

When I'm in the doghouse,
my cats still come to visit.

A cat of any color can chase
the blues away.

When the cares of the world weigh you
down, a little cat can pick you up.

When loneliness creeps in, silent as a
mouse, a cat will chase it away.

Miracles in velvet mittens;
tumbled here, a pile of kittens.

A kitten's zest for life will rub off
on the people around her.

The enthusiasm of a kitten is contagious.

An inquisitive kitten is the best reminder
of what youth is all about.

When you're alone with your kitten,
you don't have to act your age.

A kitten under the tinseled tree
puts magic into Christmas.

A warm little kitten can melt
an ice-cold heart.

A tiny kitten can fill a huge void
in your life.

Snow leopards, yes, are gorgeous.
And tigers are sublime.
But all in all, I'd rather have
a kitten anytime.

There's nothing better than a litter of kittens to help your children make friends in a new neighborhood.

A cat provides your child with a sleepover friend every night.

A child can always turn to her cat when Mommy is too busy to play.

Skittering, scurrying,
kittens are hurrying,
chasing invisible foes.
Creeping and leaping,
then finally sleeping,
the picture of perfect repose.

All you have to do is watch a cat
stalking her prey to see that work
should be enjoyed.

A shoestring
is the perfect prey
for any cat
most any day.

It's hard to concentrate on the work
at hand when a kitten is playing
at your feet.

Cats are thoughtful enough to remind
you that your shoe is untied by
pouncing on the laces.

Don't you wish you could get as excited
about the things you do as your cat gets
with the shoelace of a dirty tennis shoe?

A great day begins with a cup of coffee
and the morning mews.

If your cat's playing hide-and-seek, sit
down and spread out the newspaper.
She'll come running like it's home base.

When I'm trying to work and my cat
jumps in my lap, I think of him as
a wise supervisor telling me it's time
to take a break.

Cats put the "purr" in a perfect day.

The purrs of a favorite cat
are like the whispers of a lover.

My favorite lullaby is sung by a
purring cat.

Cats run on friction, not batteries—
you pet, she purrs.

I'm not much of a cook. My favorite
thing to make from scratch is a purr.

There's nothing cozier than a fire
burning in the fireplace and a purring
cat curled by your side.

A cat purring in your lap as you
enjoy a good book is a little piece of
heaven on earth.

One reason cats make such good friends
is that they listen more than they meow.

You never have to explain yourself
to your cat.

Your secret is always safe with a cat.

If a dog is man's best friend,
then a cat must be woman's.

A friend may be lost through one
thoughtless act, but a cat remains faithful
no matter how you behave.

A cat can sweeten your disposition
without a single calorie.

Cats stick with you through thick and
thin, and all the diets in between.

I stand firm on my resolution
to adopt no more cats until
I *see* one who needs me.

A stray cat is a friend
I haven't met yet.

The joy of my house tiptoes from
room to room on silent paws.

A silent language exists between
people and their cats.

The beauty of silence
is not lost on a cat.

Sandpaper kisses
surprise me every time.

On casual Fridays, wouldn't it be nice
if they'd let you work with your cat
on your lap?

Your cat never frowns when you
step on the bathroom scale.

My cat reminds me to slow down and
delight in the simple pleasures of life:
dandelion puffs, butterflies, and lying
down in beds of clover.

A sunset is more glorious when
shared with a cat.

Awesome: an eagle in the wind,
a trout in the rapids, and
a cat in a field of flowers.

My cat reminds me to enjoy the
simple pleasures of a full belly
and a spot of sunshine.

In a world where there is never
enough time, there is always
enough time to rub a cat's chin.

My cat is the only member of my
household who will curl up and watch
TV with me and not mind that I hold
the channel changer.

Home is where the cat is.

A chorus of cats welcoming me home is
sweet music to my ears.

It's nice to come home to a welcoming
cat instead of a welcome mat.

A cat makes all the difference between
coming home to an empty house
and coming home.

A cat on the porch makes
a house a home.

You may think it's your house
but your cat knows it's his.

Humans travel throughout the world
seeking comfort, usefulness, and security.
A cat is so clever she finds it all at home.

When things go bump in the night, it's
nice to know it's just the cat exploring
the garbage.

A new cat will turn your house
upside down and at the same
time make everything seem right.

I've often found that the best part of a
vacation is coming home to my cats.

When I return home from vacation,
I know my cat missed me because he
sulks for a day.

You know it's time to dust when you see
paw prints around the knickknacks.

Cats love to contribute their paw prints
when you're writing to your friends.

Paw prints are a small price to pay
for the pest control services of a cat
who kills flies.

As a rose has thorns, a cat has claws;
certainly, both are worth the risk.

Cats are good at climbing stone walls,
even the walls we build around ourselves.

My cat is a much better climber than I,
so I wish she'd learn how to string
the Christmas lights.

Your cat can teach you how to enjoy
the luxury of silence.

Sometimes all you want after a long
day's work is quiet and your cat.

An insistent cat provides an excellent
excuse to say good-bye to longwinded
telephone friends.

God must have been pleased with
the creation of cats. After all,
He gave them nine lives.

Nine lives added to my one life
makes a perfect ten.

Some days I'm glad I'm not a cat.
One life is quite enough.

Nine lives fly quickly by.
Take time to pet your cat.

Even with nine lives,
cats are never with us long enough.

Cat whiskers are so sensitive, they can find their way through the narrowest crack in a broken heart.

Cats carry tickles on their whiskers.

The electricity is so strong between me and my cats, sometimes I get shocked when we rub noses.

Cats have amazingly keen ears but go
conveniently deaf when you call.

Your cat can make a statement with
her ears and you know exactly
what she means.

Mother Nature set her jewels
in the eyes of cats.

Cats have incredible vision—
but they never see your flaws.

Cats are better than any vice. They're not fattening, dangerous, or expensive. However, they can be addictive.

There are hundreds of good reasons for having a cat, but all you need is one.

Cats are like fish hooks: They get under your skin quite easily and are removed only with great pain.

Many people will stop to pet a gorgeous, healthy cat. True cat lovers, however, will go out of their way to stop and pet a sickly, feline stray.

No matter how many cats you have, you're still drawn to the pet store window.

Cat lovers keep Kodak in business.

Just say "cat" and a cat lover smiles.

Cats never borrow money,
but they will steal your heart.

Lessons I learned from my cat:

1) Silently survey every situation.
2) Explore unconventional uses for everyday items (for example, a punch bowl makes a cozy bed).
3) Hold your head high and walk proud when you want to impress people.
4) There is a time for prudence and a time for wild abandon.

I've learned from my cat that it is best
to lick your wounds in private.

Watching a kitten attack a seasoned
tomcat reminds me of lessons I learned
when I was young and foolish.

You can learn from a cat how to
grow old gracefully.

You can save a fortune talking to
your cat instead of a psychiatrist.

A person who manages to understand
a cat is qualified to understand
most anything else.

My cat taught me it's easier to make
friends if you keep your claws sheathed.

Sometimes it pays to go out on a limb,
if that's where the cat is.

To learn how to relax, study a cat—
sprawled upside down, legs askew,
every inch of muscle relaxed.

I've learned the secret of success
from my cat: Follow your instincts.

A blade of grass, the song of a bird,
a butterfly fluttering at a flower . . .
I can see and hear more clearly
when I'm with my cat.

Down on the floor with my cat,
I gain a whole new perspective on life.

My cat taught me that just because
you have sharp claws doesn't mean
you have to show them.

My cat keeps telling me it is okay
to pamper myself.

My cat follows all my mother's advice:
"Wash your hands,
eat slowly,
get some rest . . ."

Comfort and cleanliness seem to be a
cat's top priorities. Perhaps I should
rearrange mine.

If laughter speeds healing
as I've recently read,
I'd prescribe two kittens
be tucked in your bed.

Petting a cat may not seem like
strenuous exercise, but it's proven
to be good for the heart.

Cats won't add years to your life, but
they'll definitely add life to your years.

A cat can lower your blood pressure
by exercising your heart.

Cats from A to Z:

Alert, *Balanced,* Capricious, *Dexterous,*
Elegant, *Fastidious,* Graceful, *Harmonic,*
Inquisitive, *Jealous,* Kind, *Loving,*
Mysterious, *Noble,* Obstinate, *Prolific,*
Quiet, *Retiring,* Stealthy, *Telepathic,*
Unassuming, *Voracious,* Whimsical,
Xenophobic, Yowling, *Zany.*

F—Fastidious
E—Elegant
L—Lazy
I—Inquisitive
N—Noble
E—Elusive

A thing of beauty, strength, and grace
lies behind that whiskered face.

I wish all my friends had the qualities
of my cat: dignity, grace, affection,
loyalty, forgiveness. . . .

After being around idiots all day,
I welcome the intelligent company
of my cats.

My cat taught me that when the door of opportunity slams in your face, hang on to the screen until they let you in.

A gray cat once reminded me that not all things are black and white.

In the United Kingdom, they say a black cat brings good luck. In Canada and Japan, it is tricolored cats. What a great excuse to get one of each!

Cats are the only pets
that bring you presents.

In this world of advanced technology
and constant change, no one has yet
improved on the cat.

They'll never build a better mousetrap.

You will never be able to have everything
you want. Be content to have what is
yours with your favorite cat.

People need to value their cat's
independence as much as they
value their own.

Cats create the illusion of being at our
mercy while all along we're at theirs.

No TV show can entertain you like a cat
with a box of ribbons and bows.

Solitaire on the computer becomes an
interactive game when the cat decides to
chase the pointer.

I never knew a roll of toilet paper could
be so entertaining until I got a cat.

On a lazy day, the perfect entertainment is watching a kitten stalking dust bunnies and catching them on his whiskers.

A cat is always ready to be your partner in leisure.

Cats are the world's least expensive form of entertainment.

Strange concertos have been played by cats walking across the keys of a baby grand piano.

Cats are like music. It's foolish to try to explain their worth to those who don't appreciate them.

Some people see the glass as half empty,
some as half full. I look for the cat
who drank the water.

Love may make the world go round,
but cats add an extra spin.

With my cat, I don't need an alarm clock.
I just wish I could figure out how to turn
her off on the weekends.

Sometimes my cat senses I'm stressed-
out and takes the phone off the hook.

Sunday afternoons were created
for catnaps.

Cats are living proof that the best things come in little packages—and they love playing with the ribbon.

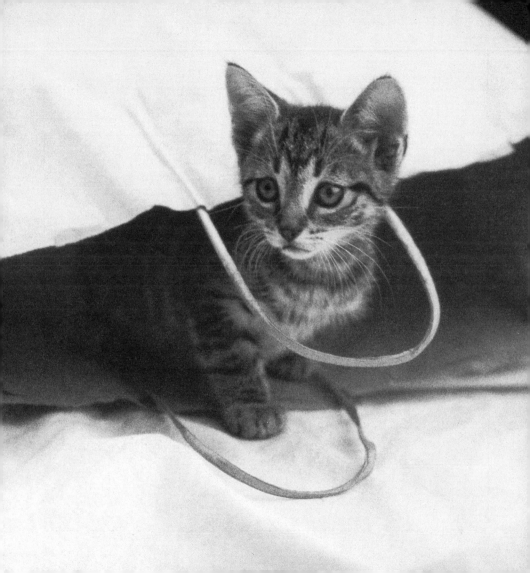

Prima Donnas

All the world is a stage,
and cats are the prima donnas.

Sometimes it's hard not to envy your cat,
doing what he likes, when he likes,
as much as he likes.

You have to understand:
Your cat thinks *he* owns *you!*

Between and around my feet you go,
rubbing soft cheeks against my leg
in figure eights, but I don't know—
do you want me or my scrambled egg?

My cat knows I pet him at my convenience, so he makes it convenient by sprawling in the middle of whatever I am doing.

My cat appreciates a good book as much as I do. She climbs onto my lap whenever I pick one up.

My cat likes to keep up on the news. She plops in the middle of the paper whenever I spread it out to read.

Man rules over all the earth, with the
exception of women and cats.

Cats may not come running every time
they're called, but they always take a
message and get back to you.

Some cats act like they're doing you a
favor by letting you pet them.
Perhaps they are.

If I ever have to look for a new job,
I can honestly say I have experience
as a doorman.

How is it that a cat can always
anticipate where you're going to sit
and beat you to the seat?

Seeing my cat lord over the neighbors'
hound, I'm reminded that brains
are better than brawn.

Marmalade on your buttered toast
is not what you want
when Marmalade is a cat.

My cat is more meticulous in grooming
than any teenage girl, but at least she
doesn't hog the bathroom while she
goes through her routine.

Cats top everything! (My dresser,
the counters, the window sills. . . .)

Cats make beautiful hood ornaments
(as long as you're parked
in the driveway).

I find tiny paw prints on a freshly
washed car rather decorative.

When I look in the kitchen cabinet,
I find that the cat has more choices
for lunch than I do.

A spoonful of tuna makes
the medicine go down.

Cats, like fine wine,
grow mellow with age.

My cat seems to know just when
I need a little loving.

A brush against your leg,
like a gentle kiss on the cheek,
is a quiet reminder of your cat's love.

A cat knows you love her by the things
you do, not by the things you say.

When you spoil a child you're repaid
with grief. When you spoil a cat you're
repaid with pleasure.

My cats are as close as family,
and not nearly as embarrassing.

Never talk to strangers or pick up hitchhikers, and beware of scam artists. But you never have to worry about intentions when you take in a homeless cat.

Noise and activity cannot break my concentration, but should a cat slip silently past my window, I lose my train of thought.

It's nice that telephones come equipped with a cord to entertain the cat while you talk.

I'd rather see pictures of your cats than pictures of your kids.

A house without cats may be clean,
but love and joy litter my home.

Sometimes it is easier to love my cat than
the other members of my family.

Cats question your authority
but love you all the same.

Memories of previous cats lie curled in
the corners of my mind. Occasionally
they arch and yawn, tickling me with
their whiskers until a smile stretches
across my face.

Your first cat's job is to train you well
for all the others who will follow.

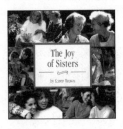

The Joy of Sisters
by Karen Brown

Here's a book of wit and wisdom that is the perfect gift to share with your sister. Sometimes sentimental, sometimes humorous, but always right on, *The Joy of Sisters* will bring the best of sisters to an even better understanding of what sisterhood is all about. Filled with touching black-and-white photos that depict being sisters.

Order #3508

The Joy of Friendship
by Robert Scotellaro

This collection of wit and wisdom is the perfect gift to share with a friend. Sometimes sentimental, sometimes humorous, but always right on, *The Joy of Friendship* will bring the best of friends to an even better understanding of what friendship is all about. Illustrated with 15 black-and-white photos that poignantly depict friendship.

Order #3506

The Joy of Parenthood
by Jan Blaustone

This book contains hundreds of warm and inspirational "nuggets" of wisdom to help prepare parents for the pleasures and challenges ahead. Twenty-four touching black-and-white photos help convey the joy of parenthood and make this a delightful book to give or receive.

Order #3500

The Joy of Grandparenting
by Audrey Sherins and Joan Holleman

This book will have grandparents smiling in agreement as they read these modern proverbs. It contains wit and wisdom on such issues as passing on family heritage and the uniqueness of each grandchild. Audrey Sherins describes being a grandparent as "all the pleasure and none of the responsibility of parenthood."

Order #3502

The Joy of Marriage
by Monica and Bill Dodds

Here's a book of romance and love for married couples. With clever one-line messages, it accentuates the everyday romantic, caring, and playful elements of married life. Filled with beautiful, touching black-and-white photographs, it's the perfect gift for weddings and anniversaries.

Order #3504

Order Form

Qty.	Title	Author	Order No.	Unit Cost (U.S. $)	Total
	Age Happens	Lansky, B.	4025	$7.00	
	Dads Say the Dumbest Things!	Lansky/Jones	4220	$6.00	
	Familiarity Breeds Children	Lansky, B.	4015	$7.00	
	For Better And For Worse	Lansky, B.	4000	$7.00	
	Golf: It's Just a Game!	Lansky, B.	4035	$7.00	
	Grandma Knows Best	McBride, M.	4009	$7.00	
	How to Line Up Your Fourth Putt	Rusher, B.	4075	$7.00	
	Joy of Cats	Kittinger, J.	3510	$7.00	
	Joy of Friendship	Scotellaro, R.	3506	$7.00	
	Joy of Grandparenting	Sherins/Holleman	3502	$7.00	
	Joy of Marriage	Dodds, M. & B.	3504	$7.00	
	Joy of Parenthood	Blaustone, J.	3500	$7.00	
	Joy of Sisters	Brown, K.	3508	$7.00	
	Lovesick	Lansky, B.	4045	$7.00	
	Moms Say the Funniest Things!	Lansky, B.	4280	$6.00	
				Subtotal	
			Shipping and Handling (see below)		
			MN residents add 6.5% sales tax		
			Total		

YES! Please send me the books indicated above. Add $2.00 shipping and handling for the first book with a retail price up to $9.99, or $3.00 for the first book with a retail price over $9.99. Add $1.00 shipping and handling for each additional book. All orders must be prepaid. Most orders are shipped within to days by U.S. Mail (7–9 delivery days). Rush shipping is available for an extra charge. Overseas postage will be billed. Quantity discounts available upon request.

Send book(s) to:

Name _____ Address _____

City _____ State ____ Zip _____ Telephone (____) _____

Payment via: ❏ Check or money order payable to Meadowbrook Press

❏ Visa (for orders over $10.00 only) ❏ MasterCard (for orders over $10.00 only)

Account # _____ Signature _____ Exp. Date _____

A *FREE* Meadowbrook Press catalog is available upon request.

Mail to: Meadowbrook Press.
5451 Smetana Drive, Minnetonka, MN 55343

Phone (612) 930-1100   Toll-Free (800) 338-2232   Fax (612) 930-1940

More more information (and fun) visit our website: www.meadowbrookpress.com